KURT**ROSENWINKEL:**
CREATIVE**EXERCISES**
FORMODERN**GUITAR**

Fundamental Exercises to Develop Guitar Technique, Fretboard Visualisation & Musical Creativity

KURT**ROSENWINKEL**

FUNDAMENTAL**CHANGES**

Kurt Rosenwinkel: Creative Exercises for Modern Guitar

Fundamental Exercises to Develop Guitar Technique, Fretboard Visualisation & Musical Creativity

ISBN: 978-1-78933-438-8

Published by **www.fundamental-changes.com**

Copyright © 2024 Kurt Rosenwinkel

Edited by Tim Pettingale

www.fundamental-changes.com

Join our free Facebook Community of Cool Musicians

www.facebook.com/groups/fundamentalguitar

Instagram: **FundamentalChanges**

For over 350 Free Guitar Lessons with Videos Check Out

www.fundamental-changes.com

Cover Image Copyright: Author photo, used by permission.

This book is based on Kurt Rosenwinkel's *Shedding with Kurt* three-part masterclass series.

Contents

Introduction

In this book I'm going to show you a bunch of fun and useful exercises that I play myself. Usually, we'll start out slow and gradually get faster, but the most important thing is to learn all the exercises slowly. It's not important to play fast to begin with, but it is important to have great note integrity.

The most important thing to keep in mind is that everything we practice on guitar is how we're going to feel when we play. So, if we're all stressed out when we're practicing, we're going to be stressed out when we're playing.

All of these exercises are like a meditation. It doesn't really matter if what we're playing is interesting, because the aim is to allow the exercises to get us into a state of mind where we're totally engaged with the music. When we first begin to play, our mind will wander and we'll think about other things, but the exercise can bring us back to focus on the music and this is a really important part of practicing.

For me, practicing is an opportunity to feel the bliss of just playing an instrument, creating sound, and feeling the physicality of my interface with the guitar. So, let's just enjoy playing these exercises together and learn how to connect with our instrument on a deeper level.

Let's get to it!

Kurt

Get the Audio

The audio files for this book are available to download for free from **www.fundamental-changes.com**. The link is in the top right-hand corner. Click "Download Audio" and choose your instrument. Select the title of this book from the menu, and complete the form to get your audio.

We recommend that you download the files directly to your computer (not to your tablet or phone) and extract them there before adding them to your media library. If you encounter any difficulty, we provide technical support within 24 hours via the contact form.

For over 350 free guitar lessons with videos check out:

www.fundamental-changes.com

Join our free Facebook Community of Cool Musicians

www.facebook.com/groups/fundamentalguitar

Tag us for a share on Instagram: **FundamentalChanges**

Chapter One – Chromatic Scale Workout

The first thing we're going to do is to play the chromatic scale. We start by playing the open sixth string, then use all four fingers to play frets 1-4 (fingering is shown on the notation for all examples).

Example 1a

We're going to continue ascending the chromatic scale staying on the sixth string, which means we need to change position. To do that, I use a "hand throw" where I quickly move my whole hand from one location to the next. The fourth (pinkie) finger is playing the 4th fret, then we throw the hand to play the 5th fret with the first (index) finger. We can practice just the hand throw movement as an exercise in itself. Of course, it gets ridiculous at a fast tempo (and sounds like Jaws!)

Example 1b

After playing these two positions we change onto the fifth string to continue up the neck, and as we change string, we slide up. Start by playing the 4th fret with the first finger, then slide up one fret to play the 5th fret also with the first finger, then continue the four-finger pattern. Now, use another hand throw to continue up the neck.

Example 1c

This pattern is repeated across the strings, combining hand throws and sliding up when changing strings. When we change onto the second string, we don't need to slide due to the tuning difference, but we slide when changing from the second to first string. We end on the D note at the 22nd fret, which is within reach of most standard fretboards. We're taking things slow here, playing 1/4 notes to a metronome set to 74bpm.

Example 1d

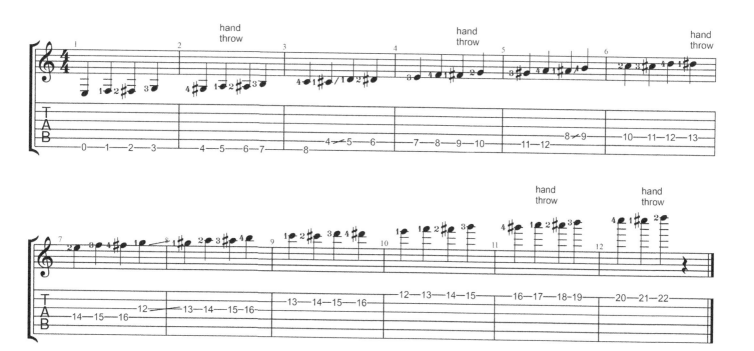

When we come back down, there's a different fingering. We begin with a 4-3-2-1 finger pattern on the first string, then throw from the first to the *third* finger. (You can play a similar exercise to Example 1b here to practice this new hand throw movement).

After playing the 3-2-1 finger pattern, we slide the first finger down one fret. So, 4-3-2-1 then 3-2-1-1 is our formula for going down. (N.B. in the final bar, it's easier to throw from the first to second finger, rather than the third, due to limited space).

Example 1e

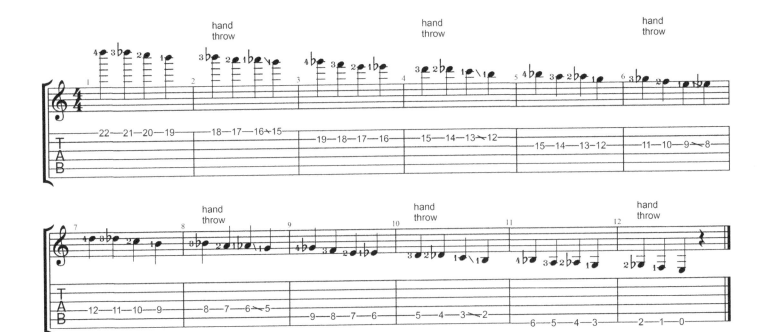

Now let's go all the way up and down.

Example 1f

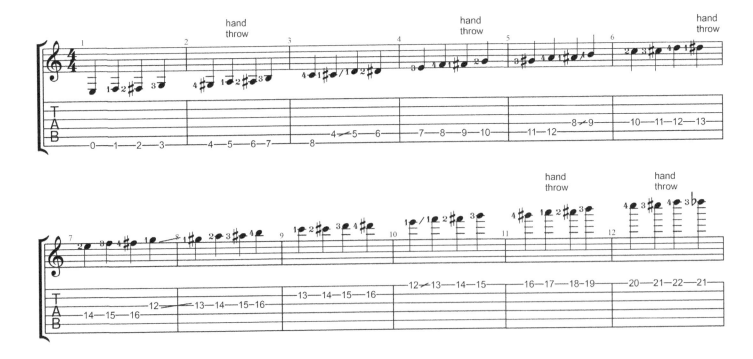

When you've learned the movements for these exercises, go back and play them *legato*. If you eventually want to play them staccato, that's cool, but legato should be your starting point, because it's the hardest technique to master and if you can get that first, other approaches can follow.

By playing legato, I mean that there should be *no space* between one note and the next. The metronome on my phone has a flashing light, and if I blink right on the beat, then I don't see the light. That's the definition of legato: we change notes in the blink of an eye, and we hold onto each note for its full value until the next note is played to achieve a seamless flow.

Think for a second about the idea of moving from one note to the next in the blink of an eye – no matter what the tempo is. It implies that, physically, there's no difference between playing really slow and really fast – because we're going from one note to the next in the same blink of an eye; the technique is the same.

Now repeat Exercise 1f several times at 74bpm and focus on playing each note right on the click and allowing no gap between each note.

Next, work out and introduce your own variations of the hand throw technique. For example, we can go all the way up one string. The notation below shows the same strategy for ascending/descending as before, but for variation you can practice hand throwing to *any* finger.

Example 1g

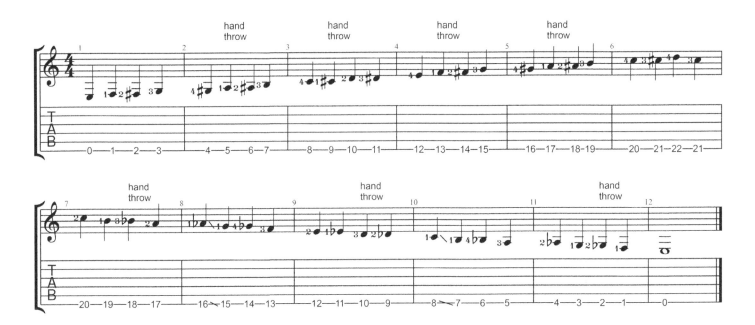

As you're playing, relax your body and pay attention to your breathing. Monitor your whole body and see if anywhere is tense. If you discover some tension, focus on relaxing that part of your body.

We can practice numerous variations of this exercise by transitioning onto other strings at different points and sliding at different points. There are endless ways to do this, but here's just one example. Here, we transition onto the fifth string early and include the open A string, then after playing the first fret, we introduce a first finger slide upwards. Experiment with your own variations to complete the exercise.

Example 1h

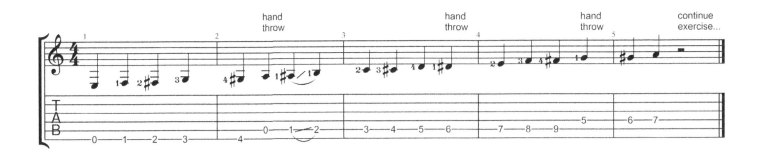

Next, we're going to go up and down the neck playing the same chromatic pattern but this time as 1/4 note triplets. You can emphasize the first note of each triplet group to help you embed the rhythm. Think about your left- and right-hand coordination as you play the exercise.

Example 1i

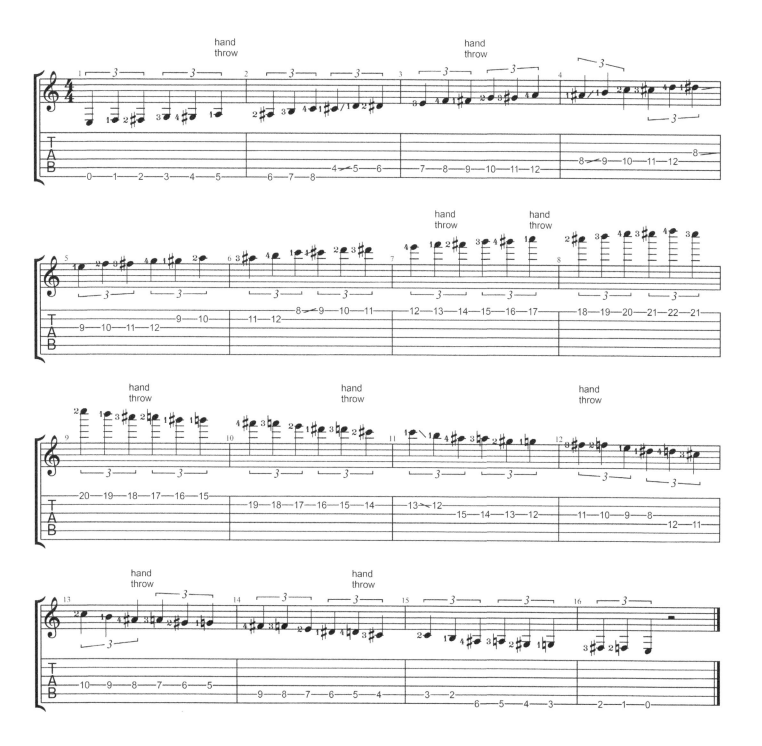

Now we'll go all the way up and down the neck using 1/8th notes. I won't notate the whole exercise but follow the fingering pattern of the previous example and continue up/down the neck.

Example 1j

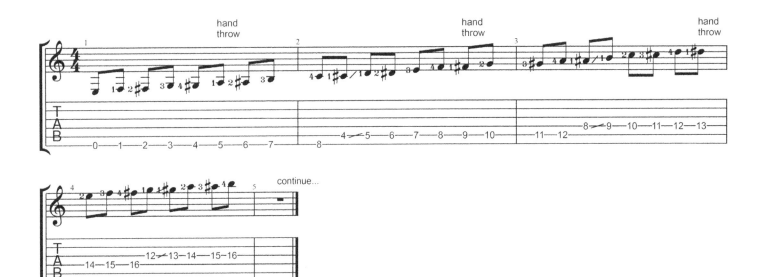

Now let's do that with 1/8th note triplets. Be sure to make every note even, holding each note for its full duration with no pauses in between. Keep relaxed and periodically check your body for any tension. Don't forget to breathe!

Example 1k

Next, play across the neck using 1/16th notes. To keep the notes perfectly even can be a challenge. One tip is for playing faster is that you should play quieter, not louder. Often, our instincts tell us to play louder when we're playing faster, but you'll find you have more control if you play quieter when you play fast. Practice this exercise as quietly as you can to begin with, before increasing the volume slightly.

Example 1l

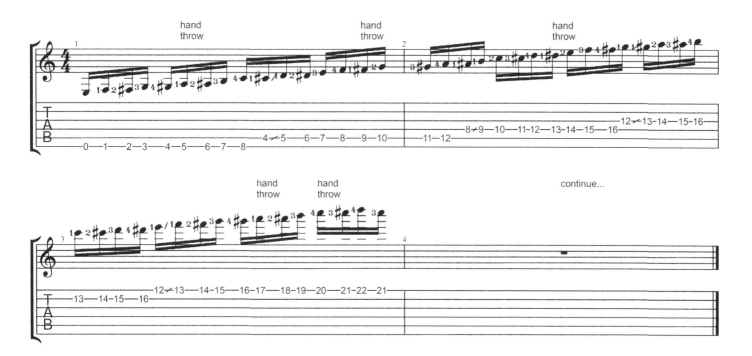

Finally, the most challenging exercise is to play the full pattern in 1/16th note triplets. Remember to play quieter not louder. Even at 74bpm, this is too fast! Try it to challenge yourself!

Example 1m

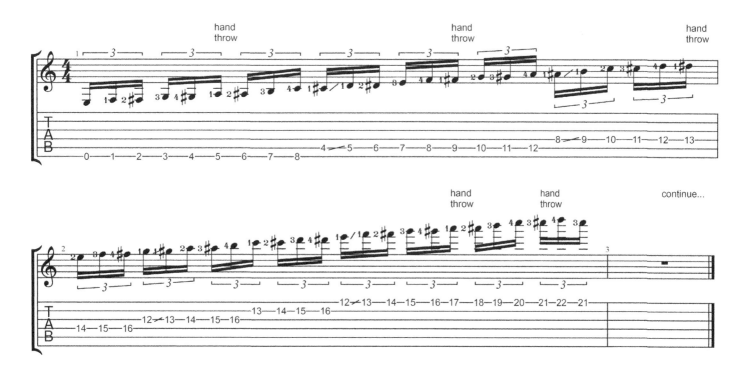

Use these exercises for a warm-up routine to bring your left- and right-hand coordination together and to relax your body to play in a stress-free way.

Chapter Two – Major Scale Drill

In this section we're going to practice the major scale across the neck, but you can use the process laid out in this chapter to drill any scale.

My approach to physical playing is based on position playing. The way I learned scales on the guitar was that a "position" was determined by your second finger on the fretboard, with your thumb supporting it directly behind on the back of the neck.

In this chapter we'll use the G Major scale as our template, so the first position of G Major, with its root note on the sixth string, 3rd fret, will be fretted with the second finger. The other fingers will naturally fall into place, with each finger assigned to a different fret.

Play the first position G Major scale across the neck in position. Fingerings are shown on the notation. You hand should remain rooted in position throughout, anchored by your thumb.

Example 2a – G Major scale first position

Now we move our whole hand up to the second position of the G Major scale, so that our second finger is anchored on the 5th fret, and we play the scale starting on an A note.

Example 2b – G Major scale second position

Next, we move to the third position, with the second finger rooted at the 7th fret.

Example 2c – G major scale third position

Now we'll play the remaining positions of the major scale as one exercise. Playing the scale from each degree means that we'll end up with seven positions.

Start each scale ascent with the second finger rooted on the sixth string, on the first note of the scale position, then work out the rest of the fingering pattern for yourself. I've included the first position shape again at the end, an octave higher.

Example 2d

We've played the major scale in every position, with our fretting hand moving from one position to the next – and it's important to know how to do that – but we also want to be able to play diagonally across the neck all over the instrument. To do that, we have to move *through* positions and I have a few techniques for doing that.

The first is *sliding on the half step.* Play the G Major scale starting in first position. When you encounter a half step in the scale pattern, slide your whole hand up and play the next note with the same finger. In bar one, for example, play the note on the fifth string, 2nd fret, with the first finger, then slide up to the 3rd fret and play that note also with the first finger. When you move onto the fourth string, you'll repeat this movement, playing the 4th/5th frets using the first finger with a slide.

Depending on where the half steps occur, you'll also play some fourth finger slides, like the one at the beginning of bar two.

This technique helps you to move smoothly all the way from the sixth string G root note to the high G on the first string, 15th fret. The fingering I use is shown on the notation below.

Example 2e

Now play that sequence descending. Some of the half step slides will occur in different places.

Example 2f

The second technique is to use a different finger than the one we would normally assign to a fret to shift position, combining it with the previous technique of sliding half steps.

Looking at Example 2e, in bar one we used fingers two and four to play the first two notes of the scale. But we could play the 3rd fret with our second finger, then use a slight hand throw to play the 5th fret with our third finger. This movement immediately puts us into second position.

Combining techniques means we can easily move up and down the instrument, using different string changing transitions.

Example 2g

The third technique I want to mention is to again throw your hand from one finger to another. So, this time start in position and play the root note with the second finger. Remain in position and play the 5th fret with the fourth finger, then throw your hand so that the first finger plays the 7th fret. Now you have spare fingers ahead of you and can continue ascending the sixth string, using a hand throw immediately after you've played a note with the fourth finger.

Example 2h

You can mix up these techniques. Just using a couple of them will help you to use the full range of the neck. For example, here's how to ascend/descend on one string using hand throws and some shift slides, beginning from the lowest possible note in the scale. I made certain choices that felt comfortable to me, but you can alter your fingering and transition techniques as you wish.

Example 2i

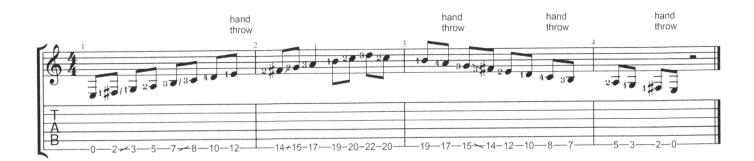

An alternative approach would be to throw from our first to second fingers, so that we go 1-2, 1-2, all the way up. Only the first hand throw is indicated in the notation, but you'll throw your hand after every two notes.

Example 2j

Repeat this exercise for practice, but this time using only the first and third fingers. You can slide on the half steps if you want.

Next, we're going to play the G Major scale from the bottom to the top of the instrument and back using standard fingering, and this time we'll play it as 1/4 note triplets (six notes per bar) at 80bpm. Notice that you'll combine hand throws with sliding on the half steps.

Example 2k

Try looping this exercise continuously for practice. Focus on sounding each note clearly and let the guitar speak to you.

Now repeat the exact same pattern but this time playing in straight 1/8th note triplets – so, twice the speed (twelve notes per bar).

Example 2l

Now we'll do that again, this time playing in 1/8th note triplets (twelve notes per bar).

Example 2m

Work through these exercises again, finding your own pathways and combining techniques. Play legato (allowing each note to sound for its full value with no gaps), relax your body and breathe. Focus on note integrity. Since each note is its own vibrational entity, we can ask each note to play and respect it as if it were an actual living thing – which it is! So, in your mind, when you're about to play a note, think, "Please, play for me" and the answer will always be yes.

Chapter Three – Pentatonic Scales

Following on from major scale exercises, we're now going to work with the major pentatonic scale. We'll begin with G Major Pentatonic and play it across the neck in a similar way, then we'll play some longer exercises that cycle through different keys,

First, play G Major Pentatonic (G, A, B, D, E) from its lowest note, the open low E string. As before, think about note integrity and ask each note to play. Playing this scale only involves hand throws, as there are no half steps to slide on. Notice that the descending pattern is slightly different from the ascending, and the fingering changes accordingly.

Example 3a

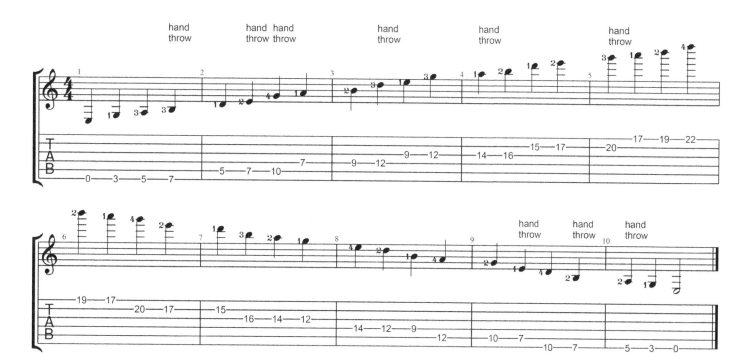

Repeat the exercise with the C Major Pentatonic scale (C, D, E, G, A). Using the techniques you've learned, work out a comfortable fingering to play the scale using hand throws where required.

Example 3b

Let's do the same with F Major Pentatonic (F, G, A, C, D).

Example 3c

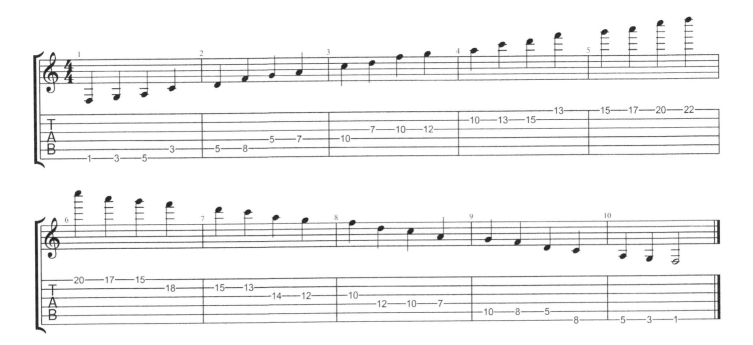

When playing these scale patterns, remember to move your hand so that all your fingers remain in position and no stretching is required. Train yourself to throw your hand whenever necessary, to eliminate the need for any uncomfortable hand movements.

Now that we've practiced some pentatonic patterns in different keys, we're going to play through the Cycle of Fourths, starting with G Major Pentatonic. This is a challenge because each new pentatonic scale must begin from *the lowest available note* and move to *the highest possible note*. This means you will need to develop a strong visual map of each scale.

The idea of this exercise is to flow seamlessly between each scale without stopping. Beginning on the lowest available note means that each new scale doesn't start neatly on beat 1 of a bar, making it even more challenging.

Example 3d

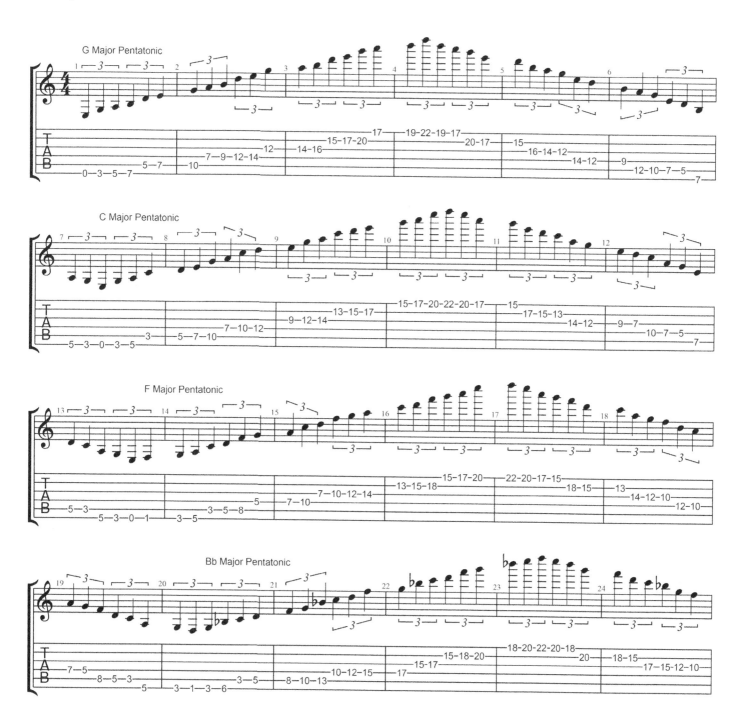

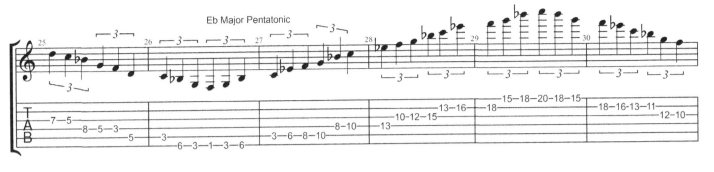

Eb Major Pentatonic

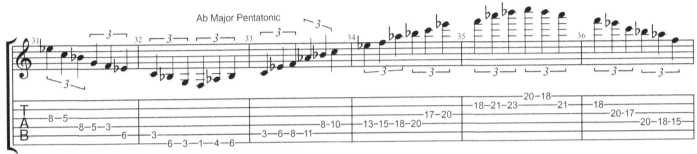

Ab Major Pentatonic

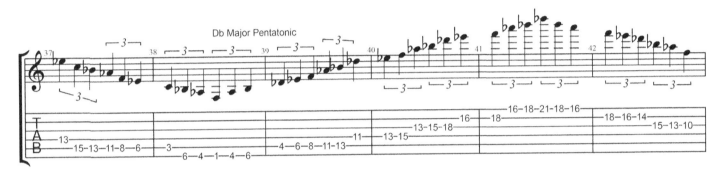

Db Major Pentatonic

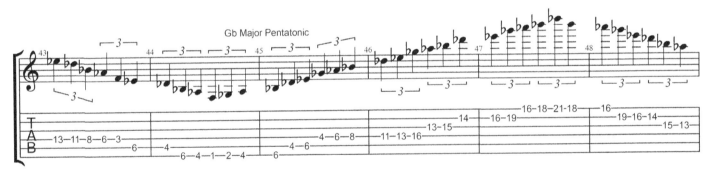

Gb Major Pentatonic

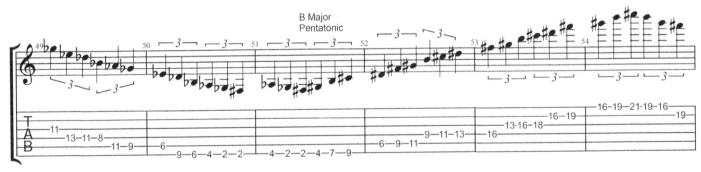

B Major Pentatonic

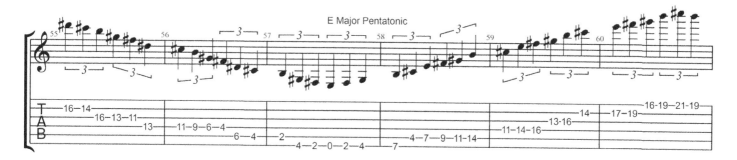

E Major Pentatonic

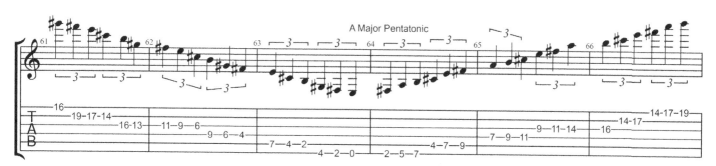

A Major Pentatonic

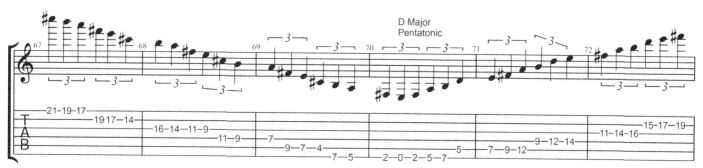

D Major Pentatonic

G Major Pentatonic continues...

To complete this pentatonic workout, repeat the whole exercise a little faster in straight 1/18th notes. Below are the first few bars, but you must complete the exercise. Look back at the previous example if you need to, but each time you change scale, try to "hear" the intervals that you need to move to. For an additional challenge, use different transition points on the string to ascend/descend.

Example 3e

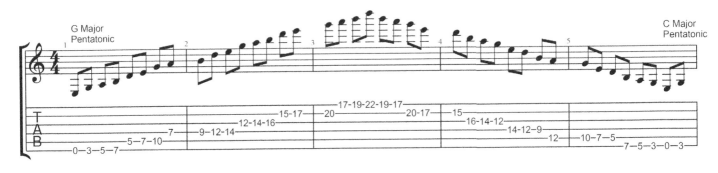

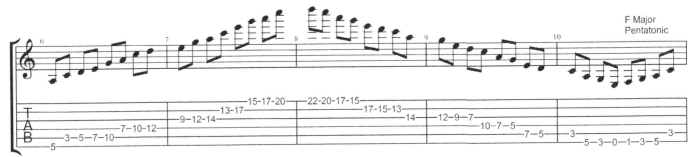

Chapter Four – Finger Memory

Now we're going to play a nice technical exercise that I love to do, which is based around the fact that the neck *constricts* when we play high up and *expands* when we play low down. In other words, depending on the register we're playing in, the space between the notes will be wider or shorter because the physical width of the frets is different.

The construction of the guitar means that the distance between intervals is always changing, and that poses a challenge to our physical memory. The distance between the notes F and C on the first string (1st fret to 8th fret), is very different from the distance between F and C at the 13th and 20th frets. Pianists don't have this problem – the finger spacing between notes is the same in every octave for them – but no, not us!

In this first exercise we'll play F to C on the first string, then move up a half step and play the same interval. As we move chromatically up the neck, the distance between the intervals will constrict a little each time, but this exercise will train our fretting hand to make the necessary adjustments with accuracy.

Example 4a

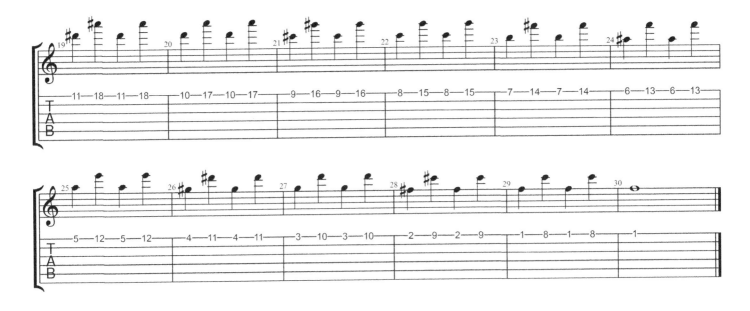

Let's shorten the time between each interval movement and play each one just once.

Example 4b

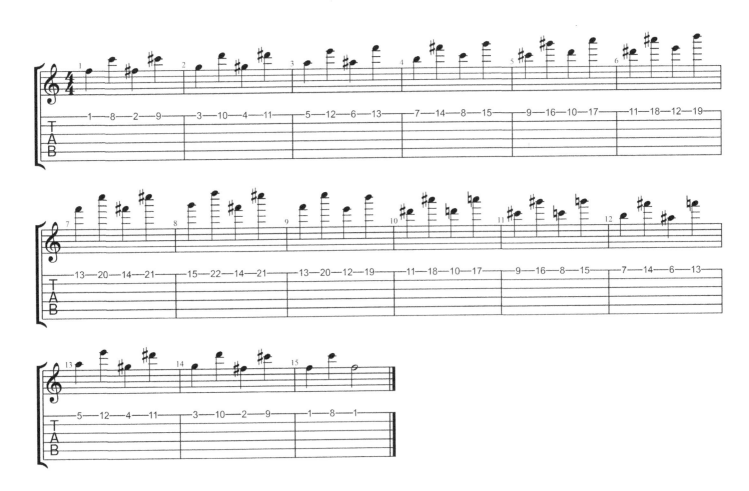

The previous exercise is a bit of a head trip, but it's a really good one to train your finger memory to be aware of the difference in spacing between the intervals on the neck.

I love this next exercise too, also designed around the constriction and expansion of the neck, which will help train your accuracy in making intervallic jumps and playing them cleanly. I call this the one-five-one-five exercise as it just uses root and 5th intervals throughout covering the range of the neck.

Here is the pattern, with fingerings indicated in the notation. After playing the first triplet phrase with fingers 1, 2 and 3, you'll jump up to the 7th fret and begin the next triplet with the first finger and use fingers 1, 2 and 3 again.

For the next jump, you'll throw your hand and land on the first string, 15th fret with the fourth finger – so this triplet will be played using fingers 4, 3 and 1. Finally, we jump over to the third finger to play the D note on the fourth string, 12th fret. The G note that follows is played with the second finger, and the final D note with the third finger.

Ending the pattern on the third finger sets us up to start the pattern again on the first finger, so we can easily loop it around.

Example 4c

Another reason why this is a good exercise is that it mostly uses a one-note-per-string pattern, apart from the first/sixth strings, which is always more difficult to play than multiple notes on each string.

Now we're going to use this pattern to play chromatically up the neck. We'll play it twice from each root note, then move up a half step. Using this pattern we can go as high as a D root note on the sixth string before we run out of fretboard for the higher notes.

This time, we'll play it to a metronome set at 118bpm, but using 1/4 note triplets. Play it with down-up alternate picking throughout.

Example 4d

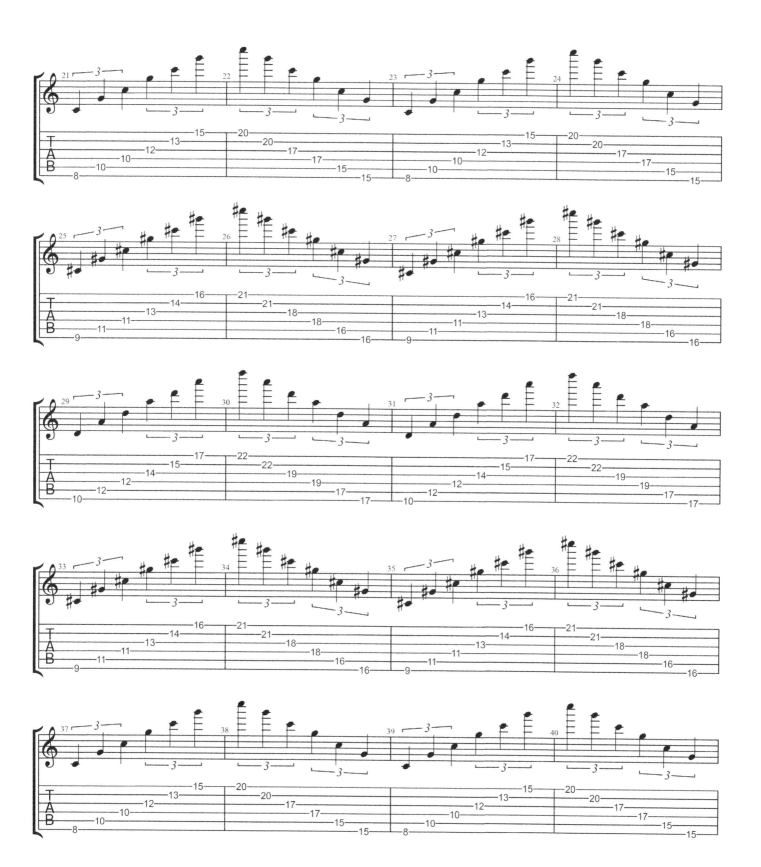

Next, try this exercise playing straight 1/8th notes to the same 118bpm metronome. Because of the change in note value, this time the pattern will span three bars rather than two. I won't write out the whole exercise for you but here are the first few bars. Repeat as before until you run out of fretboard.

Example 4e

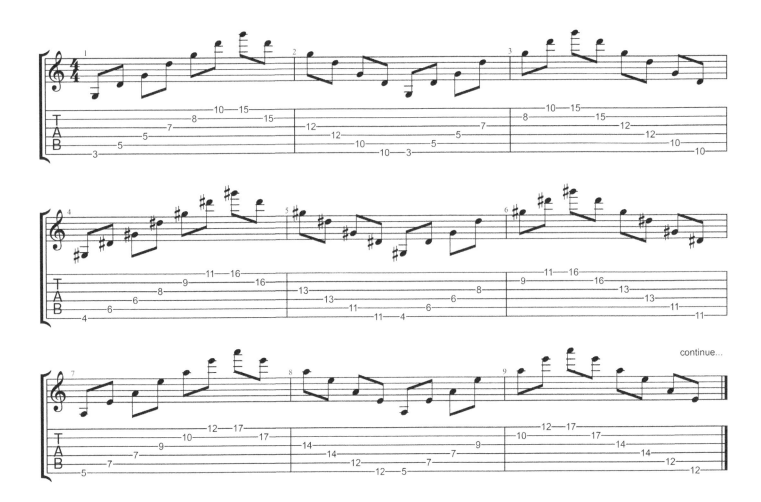

For a final challenge, play along with me using audio track **Example 4e-2**. Here we are playing the same pattern in straight 1/8th notes but to a metronome set to 136bpm. This is a great workout!

Chapter Five – May the 4ths Be with You

Here's an exercise I like to play, similar to the last one, arranged as a one-note-per-string pattern, except for the top and bottom strings. Last time we practiced intervals of a 5th, but this time we're working on 4th interval accuracy. Here, we play the root note, then a 4th interval above it, then a 4th above that note.

Example 5a shows the melodic "cell" we'll use for this idea. The fingering for this shape indicated in the notation is very important to be able to play it smoothly when we begin to loop it around. Check it out.

Example 5a

Now let's loop this around and play it with the metronome set to 119bpm. Alternate pick throughout, beginning with a downstroke. We'll begin playing with 1/4 notes, then after a few bars double it up and play with 1/8th notes.

Example 5b

When you feel confident, try the pattern in 1/8th notes at 140bpm. Play along with me using audio track **Example 5b-2**.

Next, we'll play the pattern in 1/8th notes again, but shift between a G root and a C root. Start with the metronome set at 100bpm.

Example 5c

Now we're going to extend the melodic cell. We'll start by ascending as before, then move up a whole step and descend. The fingering for this pattern is indicated in the notation below, and this time we're playing the cell from an A root note on the 5th fret of the sixth string. Let's loop it around for a while at 100bpm. Remember to focus on good note integrity and playing legato, with no gaps between notes.

Example 5d

Let's extend this exercise again. To continue to work on our finger memory, we're going to ascend the cell from the A note on the sixth string, and when we get to the first string, instead of playing an A note there, we're going to jump up to C and descend the cell as if we'd played it from a C root. Then, instead of continuing in the C position, we'll jump back down to the A position. So, ascend from A and descend from C, like this...

Example 5e

Let's vary the exercise again, shifting everything up to a C root, so that we ascend the cell from C and descend from Eb.

Example 5f

Now we're going to take the cell pattern from Example 5d and use it to ascend the fretboard. We'll play the cell twice and once we've hit the last note on the sixth string, we'll move up a half step and start the cell again. We'll keep doing this until we run out of frets.

On the audio, I have my metronome set to 80bpm and I'm playing the cell in 1/16th notes, but if that's too challenging to begin with, adjust your metronome to a more comfortable tempo and increase it gradually over time. The aim here is to play cleanly, not fast.

Example 5g

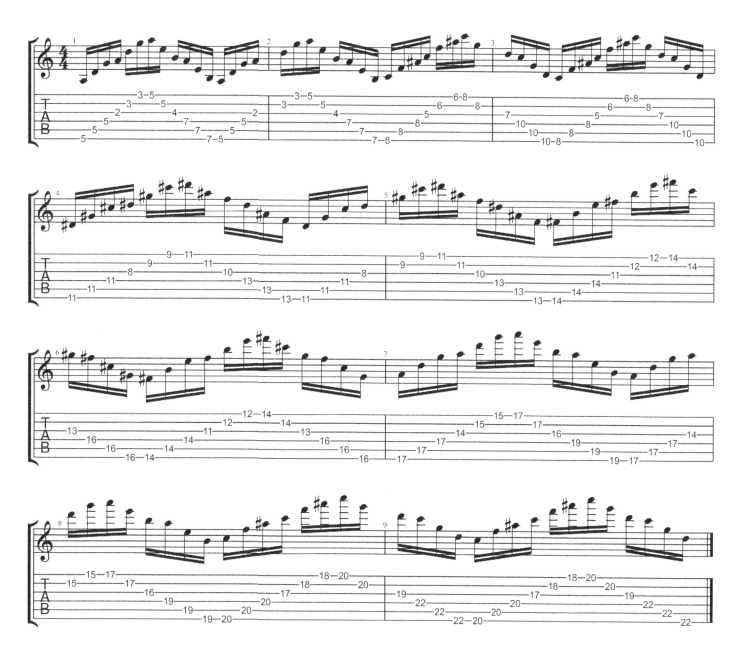

Next, we're going to reverse the pattern and descend, but this time instead of leading from the low E string we'll lead from the high E string and move down in half steps.

Example 5h

This time we'll combine ascending and descending patterns, play a little faster with the metronome set to 100bpm, and also play it with a three feel.

Example 5i

When you've played this a few times and feel confident moving between positions, play along with me at 120bpm using audio track **Example 5i-2**.

Let's increase the tempo to 140bpm and do that again. Play the exercise with me use audio track **Example 5i-3**.

And one more time at 150bpm with audio track **Example 5i-4**.

Now we've practiced these cells across the fretboard, we'll end this chapter with an etude. We can take the cell we began with and use all of it, or fragments of it, to improvise and move around the fretboard, exploring different ways of combining the notes. Here's an improvisation that came to my mind, which you can learn, but you should also experiment improvising freely to see what you come up with.

Example 5j

44

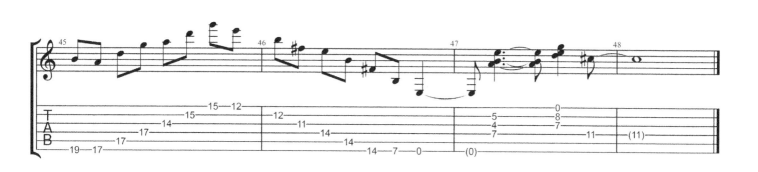

Chapter Six – Syncopation and Cross Rhythms

Next, we're going to work on the technique of playing with syncopation and learn how we can control that to create some interesting cross rhythms.

The first example shows a short musical phrase which we'll use as a cell for the next few exercises. Play it around several times and use alternate picking.

Example 6a

In a moment, we're going to superimpose a rhythm onto that figure. Look at the cellular idea above and you'll see that it's composed of two triads. Naturally, we're always inclined to play the *shape* of the musical idea, putting emphasis on the first note of each triad, like this (see the accent symbols in the notation):

Example 6b

Keeping the cell the same, we can superimpose different rhythms to create a cross-rhythmic feel. Example 6c creates a shifting emphasis when applied to the melodic cell. Try it with the metronome set to 90bpm.

Example 6c

Play the previous exercise slower to begin with if you need to. When you have it down, play along with me and test yourself at 128bpm using audio track **Example 6c-2**.

This concept opens the door to tons of musical figure/rhythm combinations. We can take any melodic idea and impose any rhythm over it. For example, one thing I like to do is to take a scale sequence, play it straight, then superimpose a different rhythm.

Let's take the G Major scale arranged in ascending/descending triads. The idea is to ascend the first triad, then descend the second one, so that we get a G major triad followed by an A minor triad. Then we ascend a B minor triad and descend a C major triad, and so on, as we play through the harmonized scale.

Example 6d

Practice the pattern slowly first, then play along with me with the metronome set to 164bpm in three time. In this example we'll also extend the pattern onto the first string, and gradually descend back to the sixth string root.

Example 6e

We are alternate picking this pattern (down-up, down-up), so the first thing we can do with it is to emphasize every downstroke. This creates a rhythmic displacement as we alternate between emphasizing the first and third notes of a bar, and the second note of the subsequent bar.

Example 6f

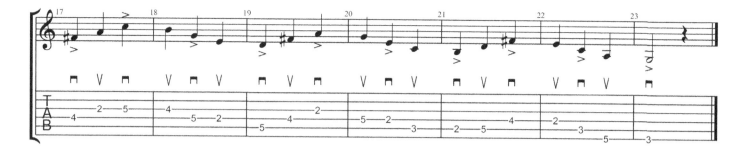

Now let's reverse the rhythm and emphasize all the upstrokes.

Example 6g

Just by accenting the downstrokes and upstrokes, we create a cool cross rhythm that cuts across the natural shape of the scale pattern and how we would normally play it.

Let's apply a different syncopated rhythm that has accents on both downstrokes and upstrokes. This time we're isolating specific accents in groups of six. In bars 1-2 we emphasize every downstroke and in bars 3-4 we emphasize every upstroke, so we create this *down-down-down, up-up-up* rhythm. Take a careful look at the accents indicated on the notation below. Make sure to pick the accented notes a little harder so that they pop out.

Example 6h

Once you've gotten to grips with the previous exercise it, let's try it a little faster and see how it fits into a 4/4 time signature. This is played at 127bpm. On the audio you'll hear that we loop it around several times.

Example 6i

continues...

Yeah, you can get lost in that world for a long time!

What I like about this exercise is that it illuminates the fact that we don't always have to syncopate what we're playing, according to the shape of the melody. We can syncopate our lines to different rhythmic shapes, so that we have two things going on at the same time, cutting across each other, which creates a much more interesting tension.

The natural shape of the G Major triads line is **123, 123, 123, 123**, with the emphasis on the 1. If the shape of the line and the syncopation we apply to it are the same, then we just get one thing. But if we separate the syncopation from the shape of the line, then we can create all kinds of cool stuff.

We can break up this natural pattern in lots of different ways, by applying rhythmic accents in twos, threes, fours or fives. Back in Example 6b we played the pattern in threes, accenting the first note in each triad – following the natural shape of the line. And in Example 6f we played in twos – emphasizing every downstroke. So, now let's break up the pattern with twos, threes, fours then fives, one after the other.

Example 6j – "Twos"

Now we'll break the pattern up by emphasizing threes.

Example 6k – "Threes"

52

Now let's take it in fours. In this exercise we're thinking of the notes being arranged in groups of four and we're emphasizing the first note of each group. Study where the accents fall on the notation before playing through it.

Example 6l – "Fours"

Now let's apply a fives emphasis rhythm to the line to alter the feel again. This time we're viewing the notes as existing in groups of five and accenting the first note of each group.

Example 6m – "Fives"

Wow, that takes some concentration! But this a beautiful concept to apply because when you're improvising, you can use this technique to create interesting cross rhythms that shift against the groove and create more engaging lines and melodic ideas. To end this section, here's an etude I improvised where I just focused on the rhythmic aspect of my lines.

Example 6n

Chapter Seven – Triads

Here's a short exercise I like to play using triads – one of the most important musical building blocks we have for constructing chord voicings and melodic lines.

Here, we are going to play a series of open-voiced major triads working within the Circle of Fifths. We're starting with a G chord, so the second chord in the sequence is going to be a C. With every chord change we make, we need to ask ourselves what is the least movement we can make in order to change chord. We'll be looking for common notes in the chords to help us do that, so some triads will be played from the root and others will be played as inversions.

In Example 7a, to move from G to C with minimal movement, we can leave the G on the sixth string in place, then raise the open D string to E, and the open B string to C, to play a C major triad inversion.

Next, we move from C to F. An F major triad contains a C note, so we can keep that in place. Then we'll move the E note up a half step to F, and the G will go up to A to give us an F major triad inversion.

Example 7a

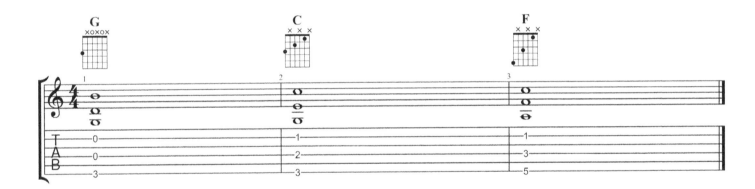

We'll continue with this idea of only moving the notes we have to, and ascend the neck as far as we can go. Let's practice this slowly at 50bpm and change chords every two beats. We'll begin on G and go up to Eb.

Example 7b

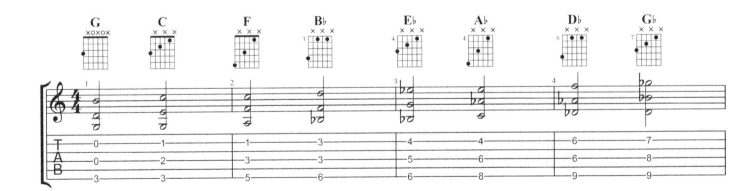

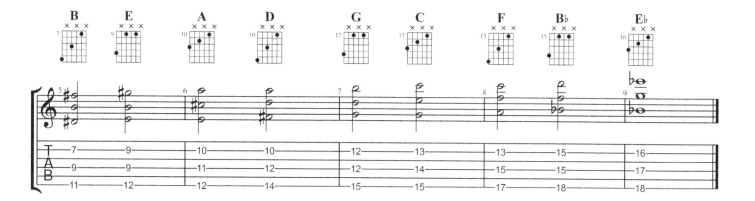

Now let's flip the exercise around. Although we're playing the same chords, we're effectively descending through the Cycle of Fourths this time.

Example 7c

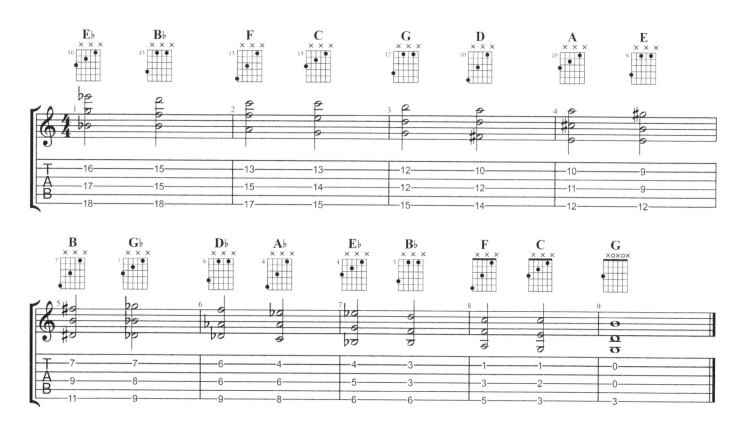

Practice ascending and descending these triads in a loop at 50bpm.

Now, keeping the tempo the same, let's change chord on every beat.

Example 7d

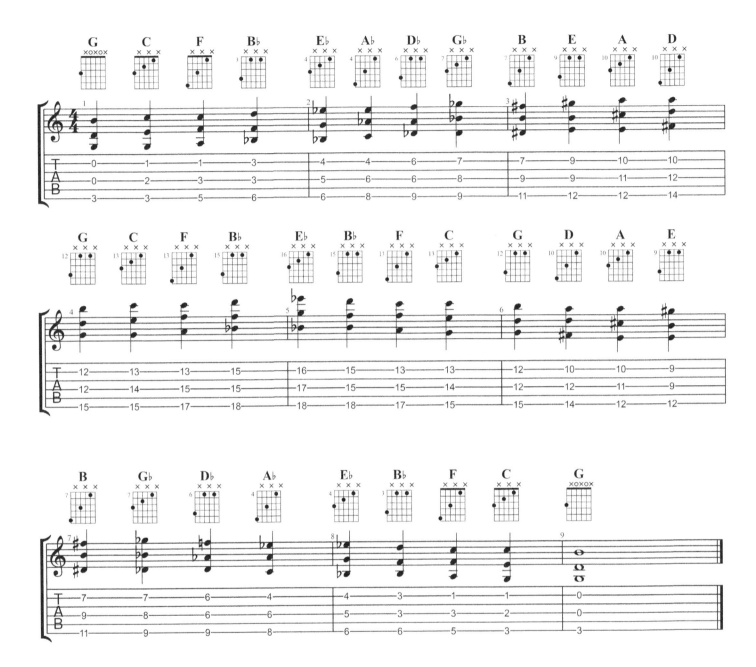

To finish, try that exercise a little faster at 78bpm and play along with me using audio track **Example 7d-1**. We're still playing one chord per beat and this time we'll also loop around and play it a couple of times.

Chapter Eight – Triad Combinations

Let's continue with our triads theme. Something I like to do is to take two triads and make a hybrid six-note scale from them. For example, let's take G major and Db major triads. Played across the neck, we can alternate them to create this sound.

Example 8a

Here's the same idea expressed as triad chord voicings.

Example 8b

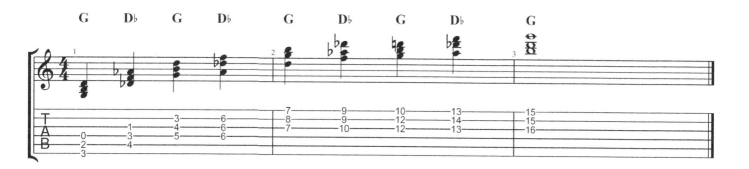

This is a familiar sound and lines based on this triad pair can sound cool when played over a G7 chord, where we get the main chord tones plus this b5 vibe. But we can do a lot more with these two triads.

First, let's play them up the neck and alternate the triads with closed voicings arranged on the bottom three strings. As we did in the previous chapter, we're looking for any note on the sixth string that's in the triad as we ascend, which means we'll often play inversions of the triads to continue the pattern. Let's ascend and descend at 78bpm with two beats per chord.

Example 8c

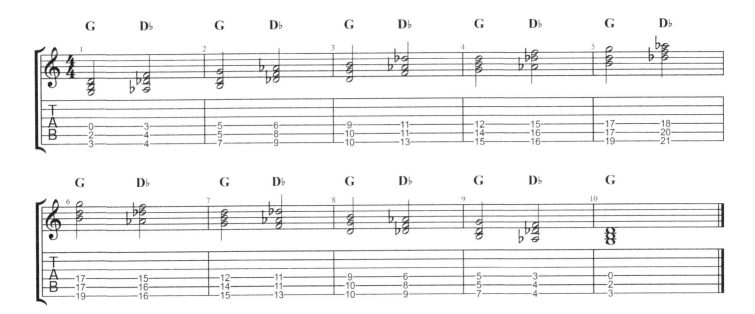

Now we're going to move this idea onto the next string set. Moving the G major triad across a string means that we begin with an inversion, with its B note in the bass.

Example 8d

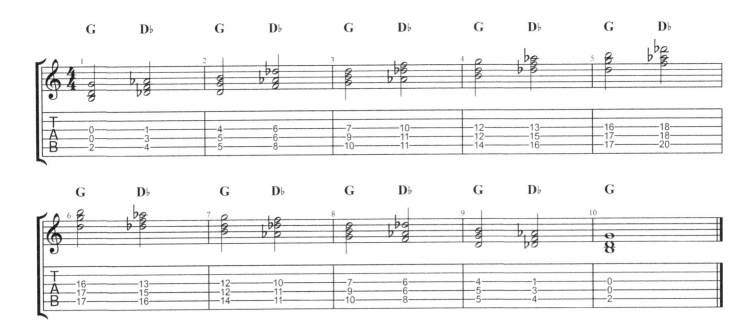

Let's move onto the D, G, and B string set.

Example 8e

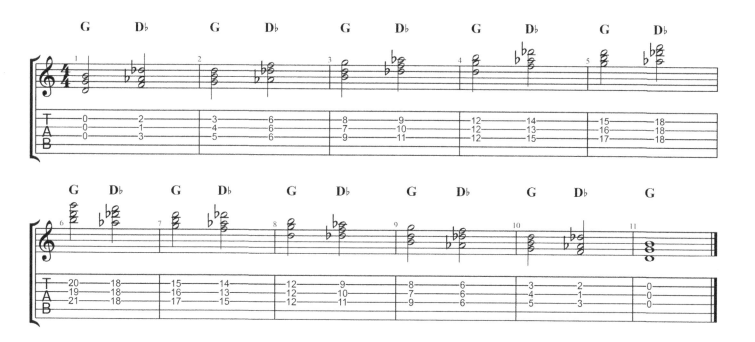

To complete the exercise we'll play the triads on the top three strings. The lowest triad that is possible on this string set is the Db triad, so we'll start there.

Example 8f

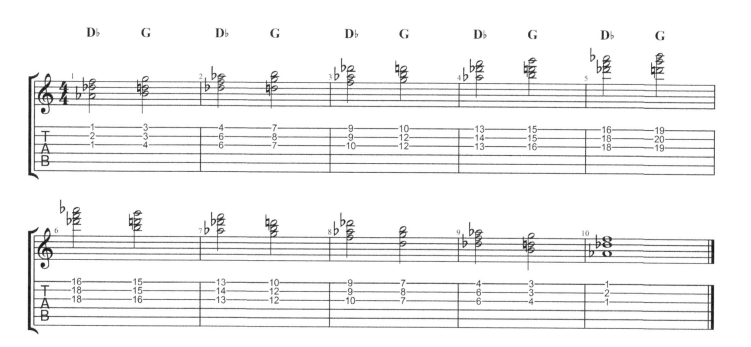

OK, we've just played every closed position triad on the neck for G major and Db major. Now, we can play these triads like we've been doing, one after the other, moving between them, but we can also rearrange those six notes and use them as a scale.

If we order the notes consecutively, starting on G, the next possible note from either triad is Ab, then B, etc., so that we have G, Ab, B, Db, D, F.

Example 8g

Now we have a really useful hybrid scale formed from the two triads. Let's practice it across the neck, ascending to a B note, then coming back down. We're playing at 78bpm.

Example 8h

Combining these two triads we've created a *symmetrical* scale, which means we can also play it starting from the Db note and it has the exact same shape. With these two expressions of the same scale we can either play over a G7 chord or a Db7 chord.

Example 8i

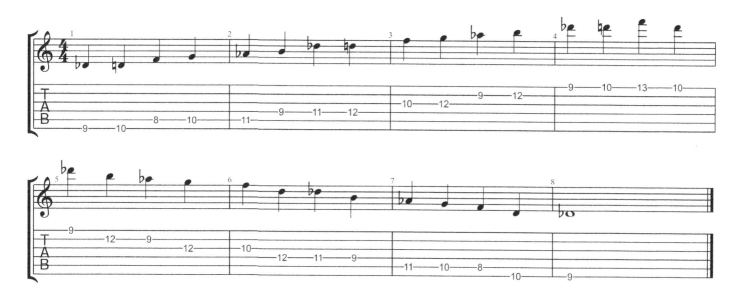

Starting from the G again, let's double up the speed and play the scale in 1/8th notes. We'll also apply the idea of superimposing rhythmic accents that we covered earlier. Here we are playing a two-feel emphasis by accenting every downstroke.

Example 8j

You can apply any of the rhythms we previously worked with and play this exercise with a threes, fours or fives feel.

Next, practice the scale pattern starting from Db and play along with me using audio track **Example 8j-2**.

Now let's go back and play the scale from G, and faster at 120bpm – the rhythm of life as trumpeter Donald Byrd once told me! (He used to walk around wearing a metronome as a necklace, and it would always be set to 120bpm). Play with me using audio track **Example 8j-3**. We're emphasizing all the downstrokes here – make sure they really pop out.

Let's do that again but this time with a "threes" feel. I've written this one out for you, so you can visualize where the accents fall. Play it slowly to begin with to lock into the accented notes, then play along with me.

Example 8k

Theoretically, we can view these ideas as coming from the G Half-Whole Diminished scale (G, Ab, Bb, B, Db, D, E, F). That scale not only contains G major and Db major triads, but Bb major and E major too – another pair of triads with a b5 relationship. Taking just two triads together and viewing them as a six-note composite scale is really useful because it pinpoints a particular sound very quickly.

Let's say we want to play over an E7b5 chord. We can use the composite scale we've been learning because, in the same way that the diminished scale has four aspects to it, we can use this scale to play over G7, Bb7, Db7 and E7 chords. These chords are all located a minor 3rd interval apart. Work through the follow etude and hear how the scale functions over those dominant chords.

Example 81

Chapter Nine – Symmetrical Diminished Pattern

Staying with symmetrical patterns, here is a diminished-pattern lick I like to play, which is really cool and useful for practicing alternate picking, speed, and position-changing across the neck. It's made up of two cells: a six-note phrase and a four-note phrase that repeat as they ascend the neck.

First of all, learn the combined cells.

Example 9a

Now we're going to take that pattern and ascend the neck as far as we can go. Once you've learned the whole pattern up the neck, we'll repeat it and increase the tempo each time. First, we'll play it slowly at 75bpm.

Example 9b

Now let's step up the tempo to 88bpm. If you like, you can add a hammer-on every time you have two notes on a string, which is shown on the notation/TAB below.

Example 9c

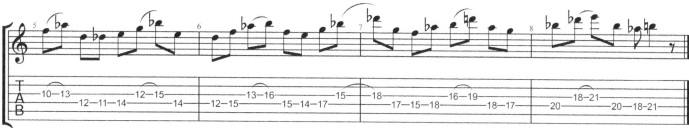

Using Example 9c as our template, now we'll play this pattern multiple times and keep stepping up the tempo.

- 104bpm. Use audio track **Example 9d**

- 120bpm. Use audio track **Example 9**

- 140bpm. Use audio track **Example 9**

- 180bpm. Use audio track **Example 9g**

- 200bpm. Use audio track **Example 9h**

- 240bpm. Use audio track **Example 9i**

- 280bpm. Use audio track **Example 9j**

If you keep pushing yourself to the edge of your ability to play at a certain tempo, over time you'll find that your picking efficiency and speed naturally increase, and it's good to have a lick like this to hand to help achieve that.

But it's also useful to have a lick like this in your arsenal just because it can be really effective at certain moments when you're improvising. You don't have to play the whole idea, you can just use parts of it and combine it with other licks. Here's one example of how I might apply it.

Example 9k

Chapter Ten – Chromatic Exercise over Alt Dominant 7 Chord

In this chapter we're going to look at another melodic exercise that uses the chromatic scale over a dominant 7 chord. If we played the chromatic scale like we did back in Chapter One, we'd probably start out by playing all the notes evenly, with equal emphasis: 1234 1234 1234 1234 etc. But I want to show you a way of playing chromatically where we accent every other beat, so that we get a kind of whole tone effect.

Let's try this out over B7b13 and B7b5 chords. We're going to descend chromatically from the B note on the first string to the B root on the sixth string.

We'll play four notes per string, but instead of accenting each note equally using alternate picking, we'll pick the first note, then pull off to the second note, then pick the third and pull off to the fourth, etc., so that we only pick every other note. Check out the picking instructions on the notation/TAB.

If you like, you can end with this wild voicing made up from the root and 3rd of the chord, with added b9 and #9 altered tones.

Example 10a

Alternatively, for a fast legato run, you can just pick the first note of every group of four on each string.

Example 10b

And you can also reverse this idea and go up. Here we ascend and pick the first note of each group of four.

Example 10c

Now let's combine the two patterns and play descending then ascending. This time we'll pick every other note as before.

Example 10d

We can loop this around and play it as a continuous exercise. Let's loop this slowly at 73bpm and focus on note integrity and playing legato.

Example 10e

Now let's up the tempo and try 91bpm. Play along with me using audio track **Example 10e-1**.

Play the exercise again, now at 120bpm with audio track **Example 10e-2**.

And now at 140bpm with audio track **Example 10e-3**. Focus on getting your pick strokes and hammer-ons/ pull-offs working together in a good rhythm, in time with the click, so that when we increase the tempo you can still play the pattern with consistency.

Try it again at 180bpm and play along with me using audio track **Example 10e-4**.

And now at 200bpm (audio track **Example 10e-5**).

Let's ramp it up now to 240bpm (audio track **Example 10e-6**). We are still picking every other note, using all downstrokes.

Let's keep upping the tempo and try 270bpm (audio track **Example 10e-7**).

If we make the tempo faster than that, we now need to switch to picking just once per string, as demonstrated in examples 10b and 10c. Let's do that now at 300bpm using audio track **Example 10e-8**.

You can incorporate this idea into your melodic lines, so that you develop the ability to punctuate phrases with faster legato runs. Here are just two melodic examples that feature the descending version.

Example 10f

Example 10g

Chapter Eleven – Melodic Minor Scale

We tend to practice the major scale a lot and can sometimes skip over the minor, so now it's time for some minor scale exercises. First of all, we're going to play the G Melodic Minor scale in each of its positions across the neck.

G Melodic Minor contains the notes G, A, Bb, C, D, E, F#. Here is G Melodic Minor in first position, with the G root note on the sixth string, 3rd fret. We use this scale to play over minor 7 or minor-major 7 chords i.e., Gm(Maj7).

We'll loop this around at 100bpm and play it in 1/8th notes.

Example 11a

Now we'll move to second position to play the second mode of the scale, beginning on the note A. This is sometimes known as the Dorian b2 scale and works over dominant 9sus4 chords i.e., A9sus4.

Example 11b

Next, we have the third position starting from the Bb note of the scale. Otherwise known as the Lydian Augmented scale, this mode works over major 7#5 chords i.e. Bbmaj7#5.

Example 11c

The fourth position starts from the C note of the scale and is known as the Lydian Dominant scale. It works over dominant 7#11 chords i.e., C7#11.

Example 11d

In fifth position we begin on the note D. This mode is often called the Mixolydian b6 and works over dominant 7b13 chords i.e., D7b13.

Example 11e

Position six starts from the note E. This mode works over a diminished 7 chord with a natural 9 and is sometimes called the Locrian Natural 9 scale or simply Half-Diminished. Use it over minor 7b5 chords i.e., Em7b5.

Example 11f

Starting from the 7th degree of the melodic minor scale gives us the Altered Scale, known by some as the Super-Locrian. In G Melodic Minor that means starting on the F# note. We use this scale over altered dominant chords i.e. F#7alt.

Example 11g

For completeness, let's repeat the first position G Melodic Minor scale in the high register.

Example 11h

I always like to be thorough with an exercise like this, so I'll go as far up the neck as possible until I'm forced to stop. Complete it by repeating the earlier positions until you run out of frets. It should be possible to play second, third and fourth positions in the higher register.

Next, I want to show you a really nice pattern I like to play, which occurs in the melodic minor scale. It's a twelve-note phrase that repeats an octave higher, so that we can make a three-bar loop out of it.

Example 11i

This idea just gives a flavor of the kind of melodic lines you can build from the scale. You should experiment and come up with your own collection of sequences that you like the sound of. To get you started, here is an exercise I like to practice that uses a simple three-note phrase. We take those three notes and move them through the scale, raising each note a scale tone each time.

To learn the shapes, let's take it slow and play them as chords.

Example 11j

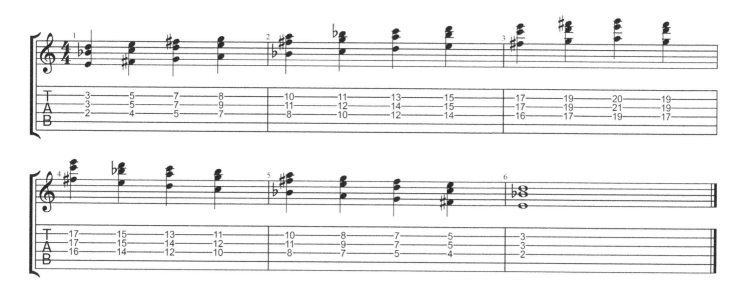

Now repeat this exercise, but this time arpeggiate the shapes and play them as single notes. Play along with me using audio track **Example 11j-2**

For practice, repeat this exercise using different melodic minor scales. Each time, start with the lowest possible voicing on the neck.

To get you started, here's the exercise using C Melodic Minor (C, D, Eb, F, G, A, B), starting from the lowest possible scale tone on the third string.

Example 11k

Now we'll repeat it with F Melodic Minor (F, G, Ab, Bb, C, D, E). This time, the lowest possible voicing on the middle string set includes the scale tone on the open D string.

Example 11l

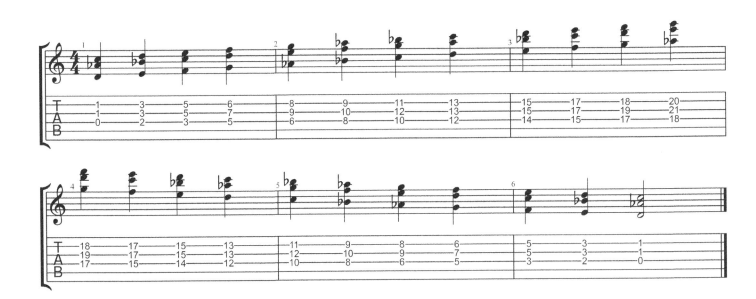

Now let's do Bb Melodic Minor (Bb, C, Db, Eb, F, G, A).

Example 11m

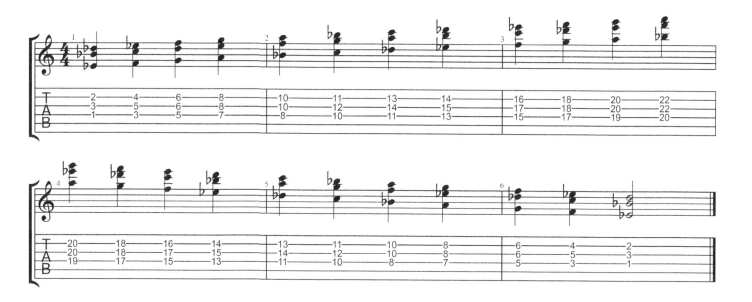

In your own time, practice this exercise around the Cycle of 5ths. Each time, look for the lowest available voicing on the middle strings. Play each scale pattern as strummed chords, then arpeggiate them.

Chapter Twelve – Ask Yourself

The exercises in this chapter come from a process that I like to go through from time to time, and which I recommend you try. The idea is to generate a set of pitches based purely on what your ears are telling you should happen next.

You start by playing one note, then you ask yourself what note would be the most satisfying to hear next. As you go along, write down each note until you have a melodic shape.

Here is a series of pitches I spontaneously came up with. It doesn't matter what the series of notes are but aim to end up on the note you began with.

Example 12a

When you come up with a series of notes in this way, guided intuitively by your ears, it's really satisfying to then play and use them as a melodic phrase.

Play through Example 12b with me a few times. To begin with, our aim is to get into the feeling and sound of the notes and just enjoy the intervals. We'll play them as 1/4 notes, so each note falls on a metronome click at 72bpm. I played eighteen pitches, so it takes nine bars to loop around.

Example 12b

Now play Example 12c with me. It's the same sequence of notes but this time we're playing them using what I call the *tarantula* technique. The idea is to hold every note you can for as long as possible until you're forced to move, so that most of the notes in the pattern ring into one another. Listen to how it sounds on the audio example and think carefully about your fingering in order to hold onto the maximum number of notes.

Example 12c

Now play Example 12c with me again, but this time at 100bpm using audio track **Example 12c-2**. Still use the tarantula technique but each note will ring for a shorter duration.

Let's increase the tempo to 120bpm and play that again using audio track **Example 12c-3**.

Now try it at 160bpm with audio track **Example 12c-4**.

Finally, let's reduce the metronome speed to 115bpm but quicken the note speed by playing in 1/8th notes.

Example 12d

This is a creative exercise but it's training your technique too. The note intervals you choose will determine the level of difficulty, if you played a lot of string skips, for instance.

In your next practice time, come up with your own sequence of notes, based purely on what note you think should come next after the first one, and so on, until you've created a pattern. Then turn it into an exercise and play through it like we've done here.

Chapter Thirteen – Parallel 4ths

Here's a simple exercise I call Parallel 4ths. If we take a standard 5th position A minor chord barre chord, we can break it down like this:

Example 13a

It's always harder to play arpeggio shapes on guitar that include one note per string or string skipping in the pattern, so this drill will help you to practice your accuracy at alternate picking through intervals.

We're going to move this around the neck starting with A minor, then going to C minor, D minor, G minor, and back to A minor. To make it more difficult, we'll use the descending pattern shown in bar four of Example 13a. This means you'll need to visualize the notes you're aiming for on the top string in each shape and use hand throws to quickly change position.

Example 13b

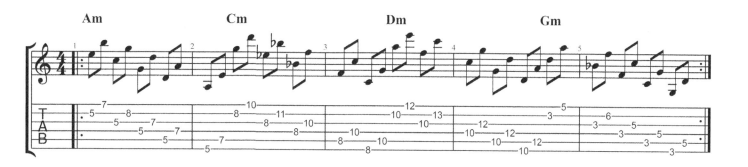

Keep looping that pattern around for a while. When you're comfortable with it, play it faster with me at 128bpm using audio track **Example 13b-2**. Use down-up alternate picking throughout.

Now let's do it going up in whole steps, starting on F minor, and see how far we can get. When we run out of frets, we'll descend back down to F minor.

The notation shows that we stop when we get back to 1st position, but keep looping around the pattern for a while, as on the audio.

Example 13c

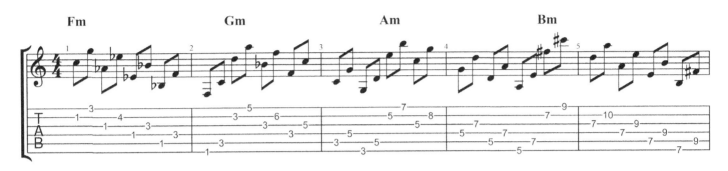

You can easily create your own variations of this exercise. For example, you could make minor 3rd shifts or move in half steps. Test your ability to pick cleanly and accurately by adjusting the tempo up/down.

Chapter Fourteen – Diatonic 4ths

In this chapter we're going to look at a variation of the 4ths exercise we played in Chapter Five. Here we'll take that exercise and conform it to the major scale.

Example 14a shows how the cellular pattern is adapted to the key of G Major (G, A, B, C, D, E, F#). We begin on the second degree of the scale and play diatonic 4th intervals (A, D, G), then move a diatonic 3rd to the note C to play the next stack of 4ths (C, F#, B). From there we move another diatonic 3rd to E and play the next stack, then a diatonic 3rd to G to play the final ascending stack of 4ths.

To descend, we move up a half step on the top string and begin from the note G to descend in diatonic 5ths.

Example 14a

This pattern also sounds really nice played as chords.

Example 14b

We can shift that pattern up the neck and play it from the C note of the G Major scale, like this:

Example 14c

We can keep moving the pattern up through the scale, ascending the neck. Example 14d shows the full pattern, going as high as we can on the fretboard, then descending back to where we began. This time we'll play it as single notes with the metronome set to 70bpm.

Example 14d

It may take a while but keep looping this pattern around until you've really internalized it. When you're ready, let's step up the tempo. Practice it with me at 105bpm using audio track **Example 14d-2**.

Chapter Fifteen – The Slide

Here is a short, simple technique you can apply to any lick that covers a wide range of the fretboard. Let's say we're playing over a Bb minor chord. We're going to play a Bb minor triad (Bb, Db, F) starting with the lowest possible note on the neck and ascend into the top register.

Here is the line:

Example 15a

Or we could use different transition points to change strings, like this.

Example 15b

Now, to make this idea more fluid, try adding all the notes in between the main notes on each string. You can do this either with a controlled slide (just sliding your fretting finger from one note to the next), or with a hammer-on, playing chromatic approach notes from below the target note.

Example 15c

Practice with some other arpeggio types, arranged across the length of the fretboard, then apply this technique to create a more fluid, legato movement. Also try different string transition points for each arpeggio. You can apply this idea to any melodic lick that moves horizontally across the neck.

94

Chapter Sixteen – Lydian Leap

This is an exercise based on a melodic idea you can play over a Lydian-type chord. For example, whenever you encounter a chord like Gmaj7#11 or Gmaj13#11.

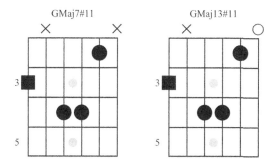

Here's an arpeggio-based line that works really nicely over those chords. It uses two four-note cells. The first is made from the intervals 1, 5, 9 and 3, and the second is 5, 1, 9, 5.

Example 16a

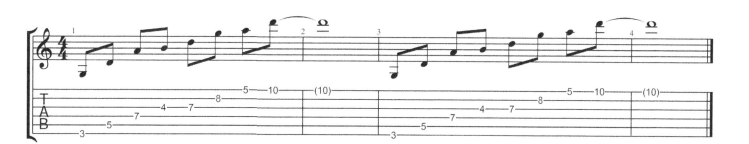

We can arpeggiate this ascending and descending and loop it around. Let's practice it together at 70bpm.

Example 16b

Let's try that again, this time played in 1/8th note triplets. I'm alternate picking every note here, but you can experiment with hammering on and pulling off too.

Example 16c

We'll keep the tempo the same, but now play the pattern in straight 1/16th notes.

Example 16d

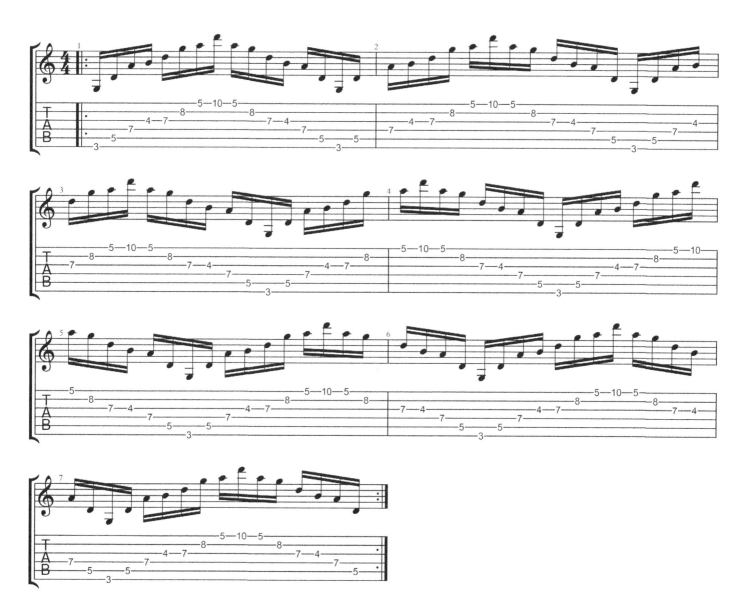

We can also go back to the original lick and introduce a whole step movement. Now, we ascend the first arpeggio as before, then shift up a whole step on the first string to descend. When we're back on the sixth string, we shift down a whole step to get back to where we began.

The notes we're using to descend represent different intervals over the Gmaj7#11 chord. Descending, they are 6, 3, 9, 6 then #11, 3, 6, 9.

Example 16e

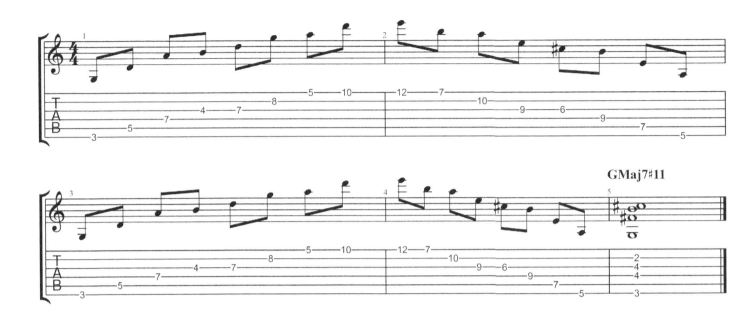

GMaj7#11

Let's convert that idea to 1/8th note triplets again.

Example 16f

And now to 1/16th notes.

Example 16g

Obviously, when we're soloing, we don't want to keep repeating this idea over and over, but it's nice to have a lick like this to use in the moment, so that we can suddenly play a burst of arpeggios.

Sometimes I like to play this idea shifting in minor 3rds. So, here we start from G, move to Bb, then Db, then E, and then arrive back at G.

Example 16h

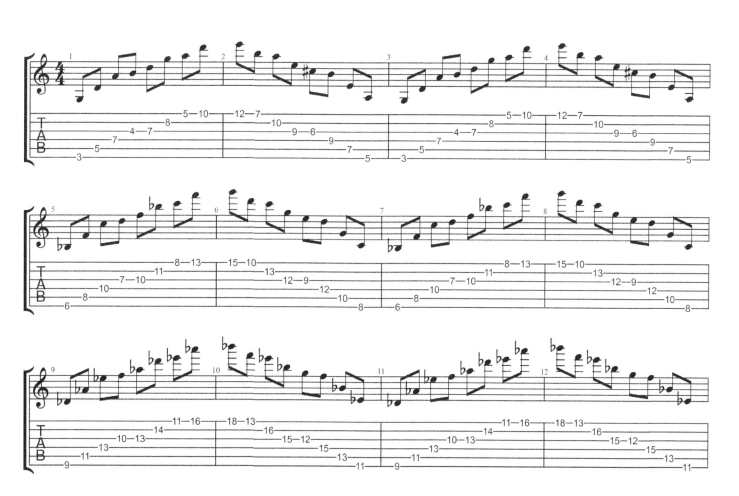

Now let's change the pattern. This time we'll start from G in the high register and descend. Instead of just reversing the previous pattern, we'll still move in minor 3rds, but now we'll pair each arpeggio with another a whole step below it. So, we'll start on G then move to F (a whole step below), then we'll go to E (a minor 3rd from G) then to D (whole step below E), and so on.

Example 16i

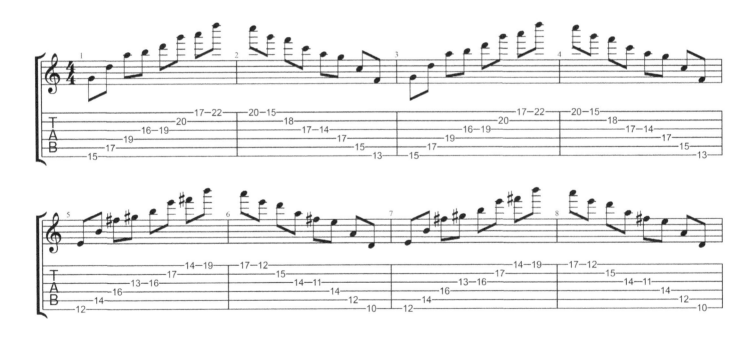

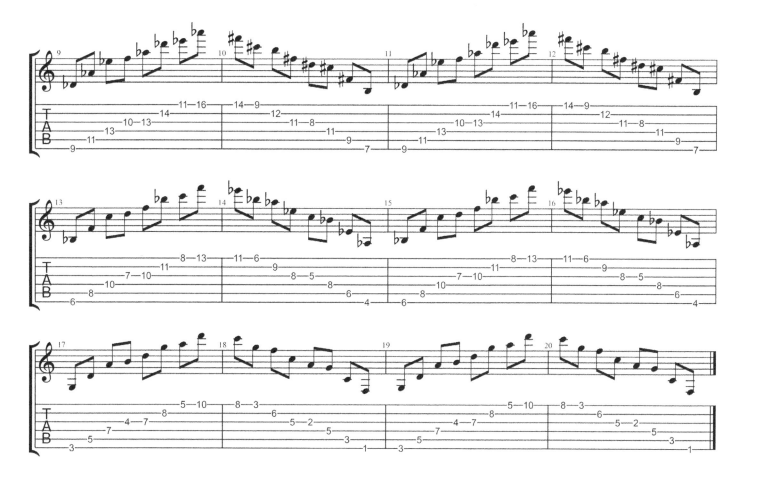

Now we're going to start from G in 3rd position, go all the way up the neck and come back down as before. We'll also change to a triplet rhythm for this exercise.

Example 16j

In your next practice session, repeat the exercise in straight 1/16th notes.

Chapter Seventeen – Diminished Drill

In this chapter I've got another cell-based lick to show you that we'll develop into a drill. This one is based on the Diminished scale.

Here is the shape for the F Double Diminished (or Whole-Half Diminished) scale in the low register.

Example 17a (no audio for this exercise)

Because the Diminished sale is symmetrical, it has just two modes: one that has a whole-step, half-step pattern, and one with a half-step, whole-step pattern.

If we play the above scale from its second degree (G), then we get its second mode, also known as the G Half-Whole Diminished or Dominant Diminished scale.

Example 17b (no audio for this exercise)

From that scale we'll take this cell, which uses the intervals 1, b2, 3, 6, 1.

Example 17c

The symmetrical nature of the scale means that we can move it around the neck in minor 3rds. I.e., we can move this cell from G to Bb to Db to E and back to G. Let's practice combining the G and Db cells, which have a nice b5 movement, in one zone of the neck.

Example 17d

Now let's do that in 1/8th triplets.

Example 17e

Now let's move the cell in minor 3rds up the neck (G – Bb – Db – E – G), each time adding in the accompanying b5 movement.

Example 17f

Now we're going to play the same thing in 1/16th notes.

Example 17g

For a challenge, try it as 1/16th note triplets. Use hammer-ons this time.

Example 17h

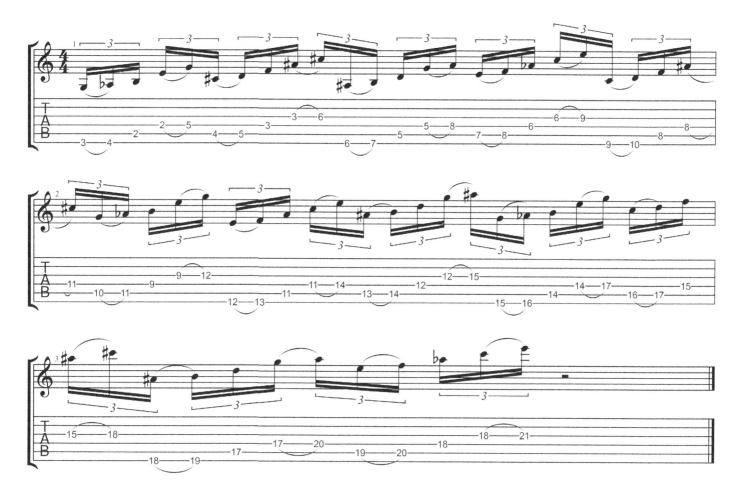

Next, we're going move across the neck using all four string sets.

Example 17i

Let's do the same thing starting from Bb.

Example 17j

Let's go back to G and practice that in triplets.

Example 17k

And now in 1/16th notes.

Example 17l

Now we'll play it from Bb in 1/16th notes.

Example 17m

Now from Db.

Example 17n

And now from E.

Example 17o

In your practice sessions, work on practicing these patterns on their own, then combining them. Use the different rhythmic approaches we've looked at.

Chapter Eighteen – Energy Cell & Diatonic Dance

Energy Cell

The exercises in this chapter are based on a diatonic lick that I'm known for playing and is great to practice as a technical drill. This lick came about after I was playing with a saxophonist friend of mine. At one point he played something really cool – a fast, repeating cell – and I noticed that it really built up the energy in the rhythm section. At the time, I thought to myself, "Wow, I don't have anything like that!" and I wanted to get a similar idea into my playing, which I could use to generate energy at any point in a tune. Here's the simple cell idea I came up with.

Example 18a

It's a five-note pattern that can then be looped around to instantly transform it into an interesting melodic idea. Let's practice it slowly at 70bpm to begin with.

Example 18b

Let's up the tempo to 100bpm and play it again to audio track **Example 18b-2**.

And now at 120bpm with audio track **Example 18b-3**.

Now let's convert the rhythm of the cell to 1/8th note triplets and play it again at 120bpm.

Example 18c

Let's step that up to 135bpm. Play it with me using audio track **Example 18c-2**.

Now let's make a bigger jump and try that at 160bpm with audio track **Example 18c-3**.

And if you really want to push it, try it at 185bpm with audio track **Example 18c-4**.

Having gotten used to the shape of this cell, we can begin to expand the idea. So far, we've been playing in the key of C Major. But instead of hammering from the note A to C on the third string, what if we jumped from A to D, then descended in a new key? Following this pattern, we can turn the melodic idea into an exercise to practice crawling up the neck in whole steps.

We'll play each cell three times, then jump up a whole step at the end of the fourth repetition, like this:

Example 18d

As a variation on this exercise, we can change key more quickly and also descend the pattern.

Example 18e

For a challenge, play this with me at 190bpm with audio track **Example 18e-2** and we'll loop it around.

Diatonic Dance

Continuing with this cell, we can take a different approach and, staying in the key of C Major, move it diatonically through the scale as we ascend the neck.

The first cell comprises the notes F, E, G, A, C. We move the cell up by jumping from the note A to D as we repeat it. Now our pattern of notes is G, F, A, B, D, and every note in the cell has been raised by a scale tone. This pattern continues all the way up the neck, as in Example 18f. Play through it with me at 100bpm.

Example 18f

Now let's convert that exercise into 1/8th triplets.

Example 18g

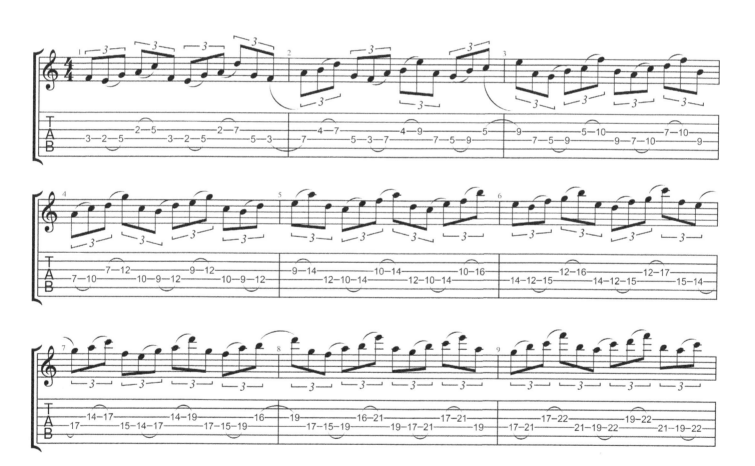

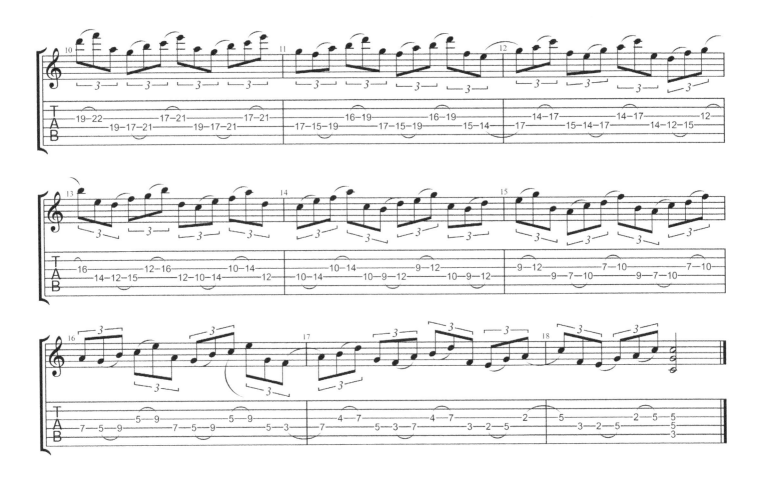

Now we'll play it in 1/16th notes at 95bpm. Play through the exercise slowly to begin with if you need to, and make sure all the notes sound cleanly.

Example 18h

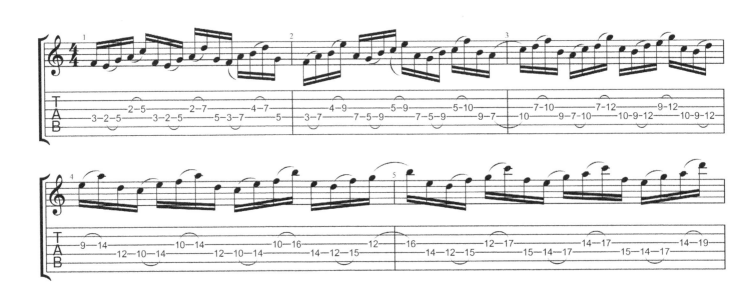

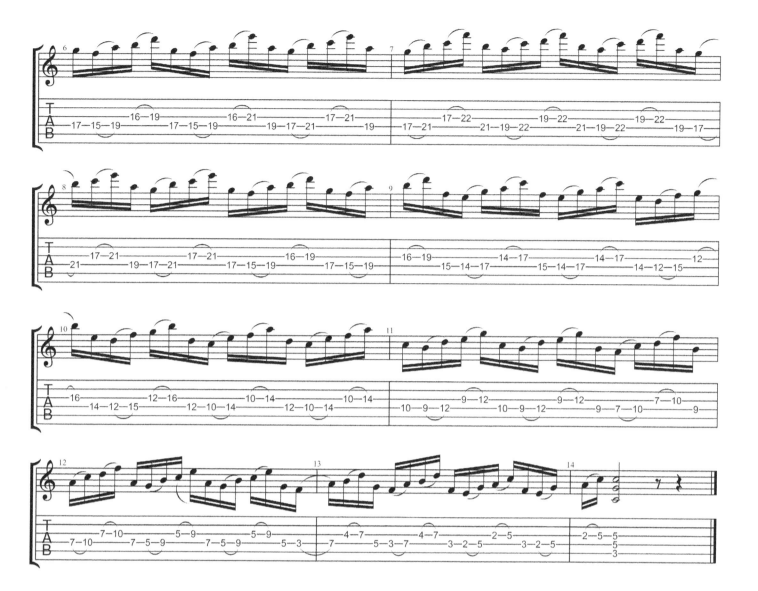

When you're comfortable with the pattern, play it with me at 115bpm using audio track **Example 18h-2**.

Next, we're going to change the pattern slightly and play the notes of the cell in a different order, and also play each position just once. Try this at 85bpm.

Example 18i

Now play it again with me a little quicker at 105bpm using audio track **Example 18i-2**.

When you're ready, push the tempo up to 130bpm and play along with audio track **Example 18i-3**.

In your next practice session, try keeping the tempo at 130bpm and converting Example 18i to 1/8th note triplets. Then convert it into 1/16th notes at 130bpm.

So far, we've just gone up and down the fourth and third strings, but we could move this exercise to any pair of strings. The fifth and fourth strings for example:

Example 18j

For practice, work out this exercise on the higher string pairs.

As well as going up/down any string pair, we can go across the strings, which can produce some really cool results. Here's a new diatonic cell pattern that starts from the G note of the scale on the sixth string, then moves across the strings.

Example 18k

Now, we can take this new pattern and launch it from a different C Major scale tone on the sixth string, such as the A.

Example 18l

Here's the same idea launched from the root note on the sixth string.

Example 18m

You can build an effective practice regime for yourself just by taking cellular ideas like these and playing them at different speeds using different rhythmic subdivisions. For example, practice Example 18m at 100bpm in 1/8th notes, then convert it to 1/8th note triplets, then 1/16th notes, etc.

You can take the idea of moving cells up/down the neck on string pairs, or across the strings like the previous couple of examples, and apply the process to any lick you come up with. That way, you'll learn to move your licks all around the fretboard and really get the most out of your melodic ideas.

———•———

Conclusion

I hope you've enjoyed working through these exercises – all of which I play myself to work on different aspects of playing and engaging with the instrument. Here's a reminder of the concepts we've covered. You can take these principles and apply them to *any* ideas you want to work on.

- When practicing scalic ideas, use hand throws and slides on the half step to make the ideas you're playing more fluid and reduce stress on the fretting hand by eliminating awkward stretches. Practice throwing to any finger

- Work on playing legato i.e., hold onto each note for its full value and leave no gap when changing notes

- Practice scales in position and also spread across the neck. Always play from the lowest possible scale tone to the highest possible scale tone, so that you're really learning the intervals

- Test yourself by playing around the Cycle of Fifths with any scale, changing to the nearest available scale tone of each key

- Practice "Finger Memory" intervallic ideas to improve your fretting accuracy and note integrity when moving between positions

- Work on developing cell-based melodic ideas. For every lick you invent, follow the process in chapters five, nine, eleven, fourteen, sixteen, seventeen and eighteen, to develop and get the most from it

- Apply the syncopation techniques covered in Chapter Six to transform any simple melodic idea into something much more exciting

- Experiment with composite scales by combining triad pairs different intervallic distances apart

- Experiment with freedom and invent your own cellular patterns to practice. Chapter Twelve gives you the template

Enjoy your playing.

Kurt.

Made in the USA
Middletown, DE
19 September 2024

61136950R00071